MAKING THE MOST OF

Reclaimed and Natural Materials

D0334177

Materials

Linda Thornton and Pat Brunton

Featherstone

Education

Published 2009 by A&C Black Publishers Limited
36 Soho Square, London W1D 3QY
www.acblack.com

ISBN 9781906029777

Cover photos: Shutterstock *(top left)*; Shutterstock *(top right)*; Oak Tree Nursery and My Start Children's Centre, Ilfracombe *(bottom)*.

A CIP record for this publication is available from the British Library.

Printed in Great Britain by Latimer Trend & Company Limited

This book is produced using paper that is made from wood grown in
managed, sustainable forests. It is natural, renewable and recyclable.
The logging and manufacturing processes conform to the environmental
regulations of the country of origin.

To see our full range of titles
visit **www.acblack.com**

Contents

Acknowledgements

Thanks to the children, staff and parents of:

Reflections Nursery, Worthing, West Sussex

Dolphin Nursery, Tooting, London

Ilfracombe Children's Centre, Devon

Ilfracombe Infants School, Devon

Kilkeel Nursery School, Northern Ireland

Treverbyn Trailblazers, Cornwall

Wadebridge Primary School, Cornwall.

Photographs taken by alc associates, Eloise Robinson, Jo Wise, and staff of Reflections Nursery, Worthing.

Introduction

The *Making the Most of* series has been specially devised in order to share good practice, showing what high quality learning and development for young children looks like in real settings. The scenarios described in this book all focus on the use of reclaimed and natural materials to demonstrate the exciting opportunities which arise when practitioners observe closely children's self-initiated play and look for the 'extraordinary' in the 'ordinary'.

The role of the practitioner in these child-initiated learning experiences was to provide interesting and unusual resources for the children to explore. The children were then given time to be creative, to try out their ideas, satisfy their curiosity and to become absorbed in the 'serious business of play'. Practitioners paid close attention to what the children were doing and saying and documented their learning in photographs, written observations and transcripts of the conversations. This provided a wealth of information on which to base individual assessments of where to take each child next in order to consolidate and extend their learning and development.

By reading about the scenarios described in this book it is hoped that practitioners will:

- Consider new ways of building on the ideas and interests of the children that they work with
- Extend the range of resources and equipment available to young children
- Explore the use of photographs and transcripts of children's conversations as the basis for planning what opportunities to offer children next

Each of the scenarios has been presented within the context of one of the six areas of learning in the Early Years Foundation Stage (EYFS) and relevant statements taken from the Practitioner Guidance (including the Principles into Practice cards) have been included throughout. However, young children take a holistic approach to learning and it is easy to see that in any one scenario there are connections to many different areas of learning. By the same token, although connections have been made in this book to the EYFS, the statements about children's learning and development are applicable to any curriculum guidance or framework.

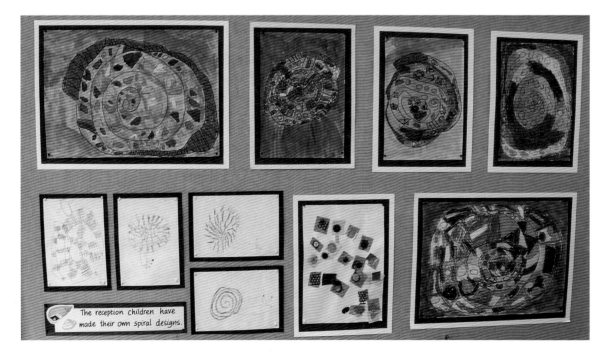

The reception children have made their own spiral designs.

How this book is structured

The book is divided into two sections: Section 1 looks at using reclaimed materials and Section 2 looks at using natural materials. Each section consists of two different scenarios with accompanying full-colour photographs and descriptive text, for each of the six areas of learning in the EYFS.

- Personal, Social and Emotional Development (PSED)
- Communication, Language and Literacy (CLL)
- Problem Solving, Reasoning and Numeracy (PSRN)
- Knowledge and Understanding of the World (KUW)
- Physical Development (PD)
- Creative Development (CD)

The scenarios illustrate how the principles of the EYFS are put into practice in real life situations. The text has been kept deliberately short and succinct to encourage the reader to focus on the photographs and think about the learning and development that they can see taking place.

Each scenario has the following features:

In the EYFS: Links to specific aspects of the EYFS, including 'Development Matters'

Starting points: A description of the context and the reclaimed resources used

Learning and development: A sequence of photographs and text that demonstrate good practice in the early years, linked directly to the statements in the EYFS

Other things to try: Additional ideas on the same theme that you can use to provoke further investigation and development

The value of using open-ended materials

Reclaimed and natural materials, in all their variety of colours, shapes, sizes, textures and origins, are fascinating and intriguing to children. By their very nature, they invite close investigation, stimulate imagination and encourage sensory exploration. Reclaimed and natural materials inspire representation and creative expression, extending vocabulary and communication skills. They provide opportunities for children to manipulate materials, seek patterns, make connections and recognise relationships.

Reclaimed and natural materials have no predetermined use; they can be used to express and develop ideas, thoughts and feelings. Children will spend long periods of time discovering the potential of such open-ended materials – what they are and what they will do – encouraging them to build on their previous experiences of the world.

By offering children a wide range of open-ended resources for children to investigate and use you will be encouraging them to use their imagination and creativity. From a very young age, they will build up their understanding of different materials by exploring what they look like, what they smell like, what they taste like, what they feel like and how they behave when you poke or prod them, or wave them around.

A selection of beautiful baskets containing reclaimed resources and carefully selected natural materials will give babies and toddlers many different creative opportunities. You can vary the contents of the baskets depending on the age of the children and change the collection depending on the particular experiences you are focusing on.

Collections for babies could include:

- fabrics: towelling, knitted material, fleece, a piece of cotton, carpet tile, chiffon, net curtain material and silk fabric
- boxes, tubes, wrapping paper, tins and lids
- kitchen tools: wooden, plastic and metal spoons of different sizes, rolling pins, sieves, pastry brushes, jelly moulds and salad servers
- bathroom accessories: nailbrush, small flannel, sponge, loofah, plastic duck, pumice stone, hairbrush, toothbrush, bath plug and chain.
- natural objects, such as pumpkins, gourds and squashes

Collections for toddlers could include:

- different materials: large pebble, driftwood, small offcuts of wood, cork mat, glass paperweight, plastic cup, rubber ball, metal bowl, small china dish and a paper plate
- a scented collection: sprigs of lavender, lemons or oranges, soaps, scented candles, herbs and empty perfume bottles
- natural materials: shells, large pebbles or polished stones, pine cones of different sizes, leaves of different shapes, twigs, sand, large seed pods, conkers and pieces of tree bark.

Reclaimed and natural resources provide interesting starting points for exploration and investigation by older children. Natural materials such as wood, stones, leaves, cones, seed pods, bark, cork, shells and sand can be used for construction, for sorting and classifying, for measuring and counting, and for pattern making. A collection of conkers, shells or polished stones provides children with a beautiful alternative to plastic counters.

As with all the other resources in your setting, you would need to check these collections of resources regularly to make sure they are safe and clean, and to supervise children when they are using them.

The value we place on reclaimed and natural materials is demonstrated by the language we use to describe them. We talk of 'scrap materials' and 'junk' modelling, both fairly derogatory terms. Perhaps we should take inspiration from the educators in Reggio Emilia in Northern Italy who speak of reclaimed resources as 'intelligent materials', suggesting higher expectations and greater aspirations. Obtained at very little, or no cost, reclaimed and natural materials are quite simply 'priceless'.

Developing creativity and critical thinking

The EYFS Principles into Practice states that:

> *'When children have opportunities to play with ideas in different situations and with a variety of resources, they discover connections and come to new and better understandings and ways of doing things. Adult support in this process enhances their ability to think critically and ask questions.'* (EYFS Card 2.3)

By providing open-ended resources such as reclaimed and natural materials, practitioners can support and challenge children's thinking, enabling them to make connections in their learning. Children need time and the opportunity to explore and investigate, to find solutions to problems and to revisit their ideas in all areas of learning.

Think carefully how you present these resources to the children in your setting. The more attractively they are presented, the more interesting they will appear. Perhaps you could set them out in clear plastic trays arranged in colour-coded patterns, similar to the arrangement you find in a paint or fabric colour chart. This attention to detail will show the children how much you value the materials, and will encourage them to choose and use them creatively and to put them away carefully when they have finished.

Creative spaces can be set up outdoors as well as indoors, providing opportunities for children to use skills and experiences in a different contexts and so make links in their learning. Outside, children can explore, investigate, construct and be creative on a larger scale than they can indoors.

There are many different ways you could set up your outdoor creative space. You may decide to:

- set it up with magnifiers, art materials, chalks, paints, charcoal and easels, and encourage the children to look closely at the natural world.
- provide a wide range of natural and reclaimed materials – wood, gravel, sand, leaves, grasses, seeds, cones, fabric strips, plastic bottles, twine and hessian for pattern making, mosaics and weaving.
- stock the space with large pieces of wood, planks, crates, guttering, pipes, fabric sheets, ropes, boxes, buckets and tubes for building large-scale constructions and dens.

Supporting active learning

In the EYFS Principles into Practice:

> *'Children learn best through physical and mental challenges. Active learning involves other people, objects, ideas and events that engage and involve children for sustained periods.'*
> (EYFS Card 4.2)

Carefully arranged reclaimed and natural materials that are easily accessible and beautiful to look at will stimulate children's active learning. Small resources, including cones, shells, pebbles, bottle tops, corks, plastic discs and glass nuggets can be set out in divided wooden trays, such as cutlery boxes, in inexpensive unusual containers intended for picnics or the free ceramic or plastic dishes in which desserts are packaged. Larger reclaimed and natural resources, such as boxes, tins, tubes, sticks, logs and spools benefit from being presented in see-through storage containers and large baskets.

Using reclaimed and natural resources alongside traditional construction materials will give children the opportunity to develop their creativity by combining purpose-made and 'found' resources. These could include:

- flexible and rigid pipes and tubing.
- offcuts of different types of wood.
- netting.
- cardboard boxes of different shapes and sizes.
- logs and planks of wood of different lengths and thicknesses.
- bricks and large stones.
- cones for wool and threads.

Outdoor activities provide the opportunity to use materials and resources on a large scale. These could include:

- large cardboard boxes – ideal for puppet theatres, dens and secret places.
- netting that can be used to weave fabrics, plastics, ribbons and natural materials.
- reused metal items, such as buckets, kettles, pans and kitchenware to make an interesting version of a 'steel band'.

Small world play will be enhanced by using reclaimed materials, encouraging children to include open-ended resources in their imaginary play. You could use:

- mirrors or mirror tiles to create the reflective surfaces of ponds, streams or rivers.
- old fashioned wooden 'dolly' clothes pegs to add new characters to the play – have lace, ribbons and fabrics available for the children to dress the dollies.
- lightweight fabric, fancy paper, cellophane, ribbons, small boxes and a range of natural materials to make creative environments for dinosaurs, spacemen or families.
- strips of cardboard, paper and fabric to create roads, rivers and railways.
- plastic shapes, cones, netting and small offcuts of wood to make houses, shops, towers and bridges.

Collecting reclaimed and natural materials in your setting

The range of resources that can be acquired from parents and staff is likely to be fairly limited – it may well result in a collection of large quantities of particular things. Pay close attention to health and safety guidelines, including any specific advice issued by your local authority.

To maximise a collection of reclaimed and natural resources:

- Be clear and specific about what you want to collect – large resources for outdoor use as well as smaller items.
- Organise suitable storage facilities before you start collecting.
- Plan a collection point for the materials so that they don't become either untidy or a safety hazard.
- Find opportunities to display some examples of the children's creations made from open-ended resources to show how much you value them.

Resources from a creative recycling centre

Recycling centres or scrapstores exist in many parts of the country (see 'Other information' on page 112). They depend upon grants, donations and membership subscriptions to fund their activities and need membership support to remain viable.

The prime advantage of resources from a recycling centre is the range, variety and unique nature of the materials on offer and the reassurance that the resources will be clean and fit for use.

The range of resources available from a recycling centre could include:

- fabric and textiles: fur, fleece, sheepskin offcuts, lightweight polyester/cotton, nylon, knitted jersey, heavyweight upholstery fabric and ripstop nylon or hot air balloon fabric.
- plastics and foam: thin foam sheets, foam 'building blocks', plastic buckets and trays, foam stampers and small shapes, plastic sheets and plastic cotton bobbins.
- paper and card: cardboard cones, coloured or shiny paper, sheets of labels, A4 folders, marketing company surplus stock and large shop display boards.
- wood: a variety of shapes, sizes, colours and textures from small offcuts of MDF to larger hardwood pieces.
- ceramics and glass: ceramic tiles for mosaics or tile painting, and small glass pots and bottles.

Health and safety considerations

Introducing 'new' materials into a setting, particularly if these are very different from those traditionally associated with young children, may cause anxiety for some practitioners. It's important to give everyone an opportunity to talk about how they feel about young children handling glass, for example, or using an overhead projector. Safety considerations are of course paramount, but there is nothing inherently dangerous about the materials and equipment themselves, provided they are used safely.

Older-style overhead projectors that have the bulb in the base unit don't get hot and therefore are safer to use with young children (see 'Other information' on page 112).

Light boxes should be CE marked to comply with IE safety standards.

Section 1

USING RECLAIMED MATERIALS

Happy memories

In the EYFS

The following statements are taken from the Practice Guidance for the EYFS, Personal Social and Emotional Development (Dispositions and Attitudes).

- 'Dispositions and Attitudes' is about how children become interested, excited and motivated about their learning.

- Plan activities that require collaboration.

- (Children) show increasing independence in selecting and carrying out activities.

- (They) have a positive approach to activities and events.

Starting points

In a nursery based in a seaside town, the two and three year olds have their own creative area in which reclaimed resources are carefully displayed so that they can be easily retrieved independently by the children. The resources are set out on open shelving and include:

- small containers made of metal, foil and plastic
- bottle tops
- corks
- large buttons
- plastic packaging and bubble wrap
- plastic and glass nuggets
- wooden, card and plastic rings.

Often baskets of reclaimed resources of one colour or material are placed on the floor for the children to choose from.

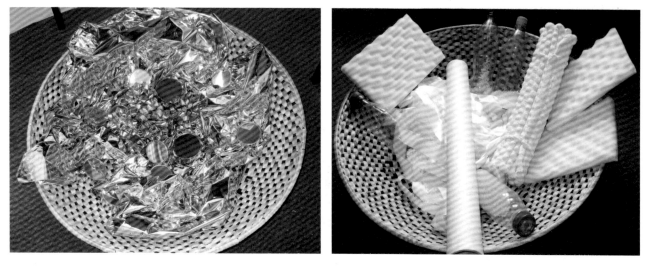

Learning and development

The practitioners in the nursery organise a visit to the seashore for the two and a half year olds where they have great fun exploring their local environment. They make large-scale pictures and designs on the beach with sand, pebbles and larger stones, an activity that the children are keen to replicate back in the nursery.

The adults talk to the children about the seaside and they look at story and non-fiction books together.

The children ask the practitioners to help them to make pictures of the seaside and choose the resources they would like to use. The adults and children collaborate to make their pictures, each bringing their own expertise and ideas to the project. Some of the children focus on using the reclaimed materials.

Others choose a combination of reclaimed and natural materials, adding translucent attribute figures to represent themselves and their key person.

At the end of the day, the reclaimed resources are tidied away by the two and a half year olds who take great care in sorting them and replacing them in their containers on the open shelves.

Other things to try

- Have a whole week without glue!

- Encourage the children to spend longer periods of time developing their own interests when using the reclaimed materials.

- Provide small containers or baskets so that the children can move the reclaimed resources from one area to another.

- Hold a workshop for parents so that they can recognise the value of using simple flexible resources with their children.

" Even very young children will take great care in sorting resources and replacing them in the appropriate containers. **"**

Working together with materials

In the EYFS

The following statements are taken from the Practice Guidance for the EYFS, Personal Social and Emotional Development (Making Relationships).

- 'Making Relationships' is about the importance of children forming good relationships with others and working alongside others companionably.

- Provide activities that involve turn-taking and sharing.

- (Children) form good relationships with adults and peers.

- **ELG** (They) work as part of a group, taking turns and sharing fairly, understanding that there needs to be agreed values and codes of behaviour for groups of people to work together.

Starting points

In a day nursery, catering for children aged three months to twelve years, the staff provide a rich and varied environment that supports children's learning and development. Emphasis is placed upon the use of light and shadow to create a stimulating, yet calming, ambience. The children are encouraged to interact with reclaimed materials using an overhead projector.

In the creative studio areas, reclaimed resources and equipment are laid out so that the children can freely access them, making real choices about what resources they will use and how they will use them. The sorts of reclaimed resources that are provided include:

- pieces of transparent and translucent plastic
- opaque objects
- metallic strip offcuts from sequins and decorations
- translucent plastic jewellery
- ribbons and strips of acetate
- buttons and beads.

The overhead projectors themselves are older models that have been rescued from a local school. (The older models of overhead projector are safer for use with young children as they do not become too hot.)

Learning and development

The practitioners encourage collaborative exploratory play in the area set aside for using the overhead projector. The children use the reclaimed resources for picture making and storytelling, learning to take turns and share.

Time is set aside in the day nursery to ensure that the children have time to make their own creations, to watch others working and to talk together about what is happening. They often seek help from one another, ask questions and make suggestions for what could be improved.

The children develop good working relationships with their peers as they investigate the reclaimed materials, agreeing codes of behaviour for their group and ensuring that both children and adults adhere to them.

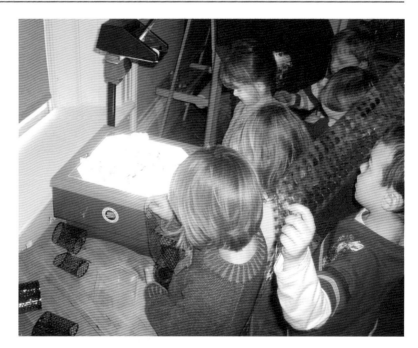

Other things to try

- Use reclaimed materials on the overhead projector to create ever-changing displays on a blank wall.

- Try projecting on to a light-coloured T-shirt; both the wearer and the designer will have fun designing the images.

- Using reclaimed resources and the overhead projector creates a rich environment that stimulates discussion and the use of new vocabulary. Try using activities to interest children who are learning English as an additional language.

Thinking about tubes

In the EYFS

The following statements are taken from the Practice Guidance for the EYFS, Communication, Language and Literacy (Language for Thinking).

- 'Language for Thinking' is about how children learn to use talk to clarify their thinking and ideas or to refer to events they have observed or are curious about.

- To become skilful communicators, babies and young children need to be around people with whom they have warm and loving relationships, such as a key person whom they know and trust.

- (Children) use language as a powerful means of widening contacts, and sharing feelings, experiences and thoughts.

- (They) use talk to connect ideas, explain what is happening and anticipate what might happen next.

Starting points

In a day nursery, the children's key person has set up a shared experience for a group of two year old children in her care using reclaimed and open-ended resources. She has provided a selection of reclaimed materials that will encourage the children to develop their language for thinking.

The reclaimed resources that the key person has provided include:
- cardboard tubes of different sizes
- cardboard rings
- short pieces of wood
- other wooden items, such as a wooden 'bridge' and a wooden vehicle.

Learning and development

The key person encourages the children to describe the reclaimed resources, which they do by using words and gestures. They are encouraged to take turns in talking about the reclaimed objects and to listen carefully to what the others have to say.

The key person joins in the children's play and, by doing so, is able to prompt their thinking and discussion.

Two of the members of the group become very involved in finding out what is happening when they look through the tubes. They are using talk to connect their ideas, to explain what is happening and to anticipate what is likely to happen next.

The key person continues to be aware of the boys' interests and to build on these by working with them collaboratively to develop their ideas.

When an adult shows such genuine interest and offers encouragement, children will begin to develop the language they need to clarify their thinking.

Other things to try

- Provide open-ended reclaimed resources for younger children to use in symbolic play, e.g. boxes, tubing, rings, logs and sticks.

- Place a mirror where the children will be engaged in exploratory play – the effects of reflections will excite their curiosity and provide a context for developing language for thinking.

- Use a series of photographs, such as the one above, to encourage the children to reflect on their ideas and what they did.

A story to tell

In the EYFS

The following statements are taken from the Practice Guidance for the EYFS, Communication, Language and Literacy (Language for Communication).

- Language for communication is about how children become communicators.

- Children need varied opportunities to interact with others and to use a wide variety of resources for expressing their understanding, including mark making, drawing, modelling, reading and writing.

- (Children) link statements and stick to a main theme or intention.

- (They) consistently develop a simple story, explanation or line of questioning.

Starting points

A Reception class in the school has membership of a local creative recycling centre. The children are familiar with a wide range of reclaimed resources, which they are encouraged to use to express their ideas and to create stories.

The reclaimed resources that are available to the children include:
- small plastic pots and lids
- glass nuggets
- straws and tubes
- plastic rivets, caps and badges
- miniature perfume bottles
- ribbons and wools
- pot-pourri
- stones, shells and sand.

Table mats of different colours and shapes, and wooden trays are available for the children to use as a base for their storytelling.

Learning and development

The children in the Reception class are encouraged to develop simple stories and to record them pictorially using the reclaimed resources. They often choose to work individually, developing a storyline which relates to their experiences at home with their family members and pets.

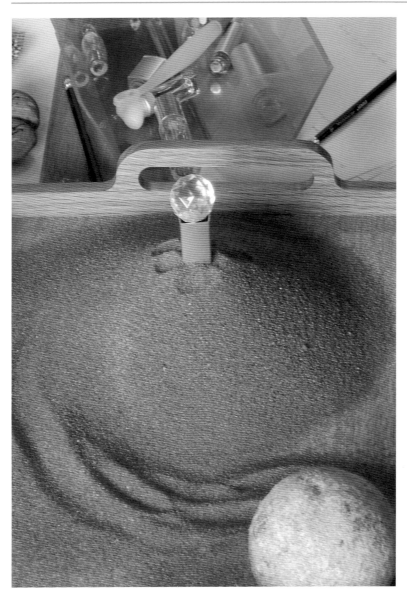

The different shapes of the table mats and trays encourage the children to create stories that are meaningful to them and which they can then retell to other children or to the practitioners.

Using reclaimed resources and story mats is an ideal way for the practitioners to set up collaborative tasks involving shared storytelling.

A group of girls decide to create a story using 3D reclaimed resources, to which they add some natural materials, embedded in pink sand on a wooden tray. At the beginning, they are particularly interested in the miniature perfume bottles and reclaimed resources that resemble jewels and treasure. The queen sits in splendour at the top of the hill. Stones of different sizes are used to create a castle and pot-pourri and skeleton leaves become the forest.

As the story progresses, the tale of the queen's treasure involves different characters who are represented by the bottle tops and a small yoghurt bottle. The children are encouraged to think, and talk, about how the characters felt.

The girls decide to place a mirror behind their tray to add further interest to their story.

By providing the open-ended reclaimed resources and giving the children the time they need, the practitioner is able to encourage the children to interact with each other, to negotiate plans and to take turns in their conversations as the storytelling develops.

Other things to try

- Take photographs of the stories the children create as they develop. Revisit the stories with the children from time to time.

- Encourage the children to describe and name the reclaimed resources that you have provided in order to extend their vocabulary.

- Consider creating collaborative stories outside using larger items of reclaimed resources, such as planks of wood, logs, bricks, guttering and hosepipes.

Exploring numbers

In the EYFS

The following statements are taken from the Practice Guidance for the EYFS, Problem Solving, Reasoning and Numeracy (Numbers as Labels and for Counting).

- Provide collections of interesting things for children to sort, order, count and label in their play.

- Note how children use their developing understanding of maths to solve mathematical problems.

- (Children) use some number names and number language spontaneously.

- **ELG** (They) use developing mathematical ideas and methods to solve practical problems.

Starting points

Collections of interesting reclaimed materials are laid out on open shelves in the home base for the three and four year olds in a day nursery. The resources are used by the children in all aspects of their learning.

The reclaimed resources provided include:

- bottle tops
- nozzles and caps
- small bottles
- tiny pots
- plastic discs
- buttons
- glass nuggets.

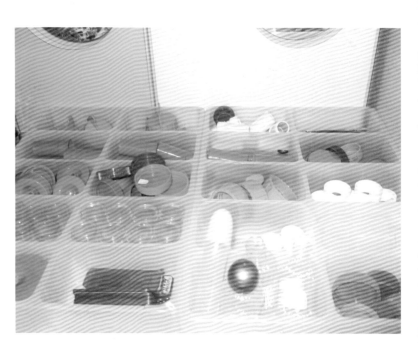

Learning and development

Buttons of different shapes, sizes, materials and colours are carefully displayed. They are then used by the children in many different ways, often to support mathematical investigation and discovery.

By displaying a range of sheets of paper in different shapes and sizes alongside the container of buttons, the practitioners encourage the children to count in their play, to develop mathematical ideas, to solve problems and to record their findings.

Reclaimed storage trays encourage sorting, counting and one-to-one correspondence using the buttons and other reclaimed materials.

Providing reclaimed mirror tiles and storage boxes with shiny surfaces, encourages the children to make patterns and count with the glass nuggets and buttons. Using a reflective surface creates some interesting counting problems to solve, often introducing larger numbers.

Placing the buttons and the plastic and glass shapes on to an overhead projector creates large-scale projected images on the nursery wall. The children have fun exploring numbers and counting collaboratively as they set each other mathematical problems to solve.

Playing with the large-scale images also encourages talk about size, shape and quantity. The practitioners help the children to develop appropriate vocabulary and mathematical understanding.

Other things to try

- Provide reclaimed containers, such as clear plastic globes and net bags for laundry liquids and tablets, for the children to count reclaimed materials into.

- Plastic trays used for eggs, once thoroughly cleaned, can be used to count to 6, 10 and 12.

- Numerals from birthday cards and badges can be used as labels for counting.

- Try counting the holes in buttons when using a light box or an overhead projector.

" Provide collections of interesting things for children to sort, order, count and label in their play. **"**

A measuring problem solved

In the EYFS

The following statements are taken from the Practice Guidance for the EYFS, Problem Solving, Reasoning and Numeracy (Shape, Space and Measures).

- Play and other imaginative and creative activities help children to make sense of their experience and 'transform' their knowledge, fostering cognitive development.

- Provide opportunities for children to measure (non-standard units).

- (Children) observe and use positional language.

- **ELG** (They) use language such as 'greater', 'smaller', 'heavier' or 'lighter' to compare quantities.

Starting points

From 22 months, children begin to understand variations in size. Providing children of this age with reclaimed materials, such as cardboard tubes and rings, will encourage them to develop an understanding of measuring and comparing height, as well as supporting their use of positional language.

Older children will use their understanding of shape, space and measures during their creative play. You can enhance outdoor role-play by providing:

- pipes
- guttering
- brushes
- wood offcuts
- bricks
- appropriate tools, such as paint brushes and measures.

Learning and development

The two year olds in a nursery are investigating cardboard tubes and rings. The practitioner supports the children as they build the highest structure they can. She demonstrates the language of shape, position and measures, for example, 'the round ring', 'over', 'under', 'on top of', 'high' and 'tall'.

The children are encouraged to develop their understanding of height by anticipating how high they can build and by talking about whether or not they are taller or shorter than their construction.

These three year olds are involved in imaginative play in the outdoor construction area, where the practitioners have provided a range of reclaimed materials and tools for the budding builders.

The children are intrigued by the materials and begin to investigate and categorise the different shapes and sizes of the resources.

One of the children begins to use his previous understanding of measurement when he finds the retractable tape measure in the tool box.

A third child involved in the role-play chooses a piece of wood to 'measure' the doorway of the shed.

He is then intrigued by a second retractable tape measure that he has found in the tool box, and uses it to measure the doorway, building on his earlier understanding of measurement. The children's conversations, using comparisons and measures such as 'bigger', 'smaller', 'long', 'high' and 'taller', show a clear link between their developing thinking and learning about size and measures.

The practitioner is actively engaged in documenting the children's learning process in photographs.

Other things to try

- Provide a range of reclaimed materials for the children to arrange, compare and order.

- Collect a range of boxes of different sizes for the children to use in construction in small world play and on a larger scale out of doors.

- Set up a building area outside, resourced with reclaimed materials, where the children can measure and weigh wood, sand and stones.

- Add a timer to the building area and invent games where the children complete a task using the reclaimed resources in a given time.

❝Provide opportunities for children to measure using non standard units.❞

❝Children begin to categorise the resources into different shapes and sizes.❞

See the tower grow

In the EYFS

The following statements are taken from the Practice Guidance for the EYFS, Knowledge and Understanding of the World (Designing and Making).

- 'Designing and Making' is about the ways in which children learn about the construction process, and the tools and techniques that can be used to assemble materials creatively and safely.

- Provide a range of construction materials containing a variety of shapes, sizes and ways of joining, and support the children in their use.

- (Children) investigate various construction materials.

- (They) construct with a purpose in mind, using a variety of resources.

Starting points

In the pre-school room of a day nursery, the three and four year olds use a rich variety of construction materials to enhance their imaginative play. In the construction area they have access to reclaimed materials from the local creative recycling centre in addition to construction kits.

The reclaimed resources that are provided include:

- strong, coloured cardboard tubes
- brown cardboard tubes of different sizes
- cardboard rings.

Learning and development

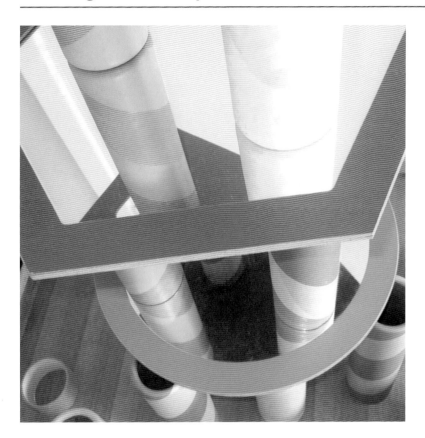

A group of children in the pre-school decide that they want to create an imaginary world for their play about pirates. They opt to use the open-ended resources consisting of cardboard tubes and rings of different shapes and sizes.

The children are accustomed to combining reclaimed and bought resources in their play but they are still left with the problem of how to create a tall, stable structure for their pirate world.

In the nursery, children of all ages have a range of mirrors available for them to use. The children decide to use their hand-held mirrors – round, square and hexagonal – to act as 'floors' in their tall building.

The pre-school children invite the two year olds into their construction area to see the wonderful building they have created. The two year olds are then inspired to try out the new construction techniques for themselves.

The girls are particularly interested in how high they can build.

The boys, however, are determined to make their structure as stable as possible.

The two year olds use the knowledge and experiences they have gained from talking to the three and four year olds to help them to build up their own ideas, concepts and skills.

Other things to try

- Add a variety of boxes to your construction area. Larger boxes can be used outdoors.

- Plastic bottles with their tops on can be used alongside cylinders and tubes.

- Tubing of different thicknesses will add interest.

- Encourage the children to combine reclaimed open-ended materials and construction kits in their play.

“Children construct with a purpose in mind, using a variety of resources.”

“Young children enjoy using a rich variety of construction materials to enhance their imaginative play.”

Into the box!

In the EYFS

The following statements are taken from the Practice Guidance for the EYFS, Knowledge and Understanding of the World (Exploration and Investigation).

- 'Exploration and Investigation' is about how children investigate objects, materials and their properties, learn about change and patterns, similarities and differences, and question how and why things work.
- Encourage children to raise questions and suggest solutions and answers.
- (Children) show curiosity and interest in the features of objects and living things.
- (They) explain their own knowledge and understanding, and ask appropriate questions of others.

Starting points

In a children's centre offering services for children under five and their families, reclaimed resources are freely available for the children to explore and investigate. The reclaimed resources are carefully stored in baskets of different shapes and sizes, often with a theme to the contents.

One of the baskets contains a selection of reclaimed objects made from different materials, including:

- plastic containers and lids
- wooden rings and boxes
- cardboard boxes
- 'found' natural materials.
- metal bowls and jugs

Learning and development

In the children's centre, two boys are particularly interested in the contents of the box of reclaimed objects made from different materials. They quickly become engaged in active learning as they eagerly discover things about the objects for themselves.

As they investigate the different objects, the boys use all of their senses and look closely at the similarities and differences between the things they find. They carefully handle all the objects in turn, offer information and ask each other questions about the reclaimed objects and what they are made from.

'This looks like a stone.'
'Is it heavy?'
'What's inside?'

The investigation then changes direction when the boys discover a cardboard box. They look inside the box to see what might fit inside and they talk about how it was made.

'It's a special box.'
'I bet we could fit hundreds in here.'
'The big ones won't fit.'
'Put little ones in.'

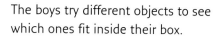

The boys try different objects to see which ones fit inside their box.

They count the number of reclaimed objects that fit in the box.

The boys then begin a whole new area of enquiry. They decide that the box needs a better lid and so a whole new investigation begins as they explore the size, shape and properties of the open-ended resources in their basket to find a solution to their problem.

'We need a better lid.'
'Find a flat thing.'
'Look, it fits!'

The practitioners in the children's centre document the boys' learning through photographs and by recording the words they say. This documentation is then used to inform the practitioners' planning for the next steps in the children's learning.

Other things to try

- Provide baskets of reclaimed resources that contain objects made from one material only – metal, cardboard, plastic or wood – for the children to investigate.

- Use reclaimed objects made from different materials in the water tray to investigate floating and sinking.

- Include a magnet in your basket of reclaimed resources to provoke further investigation.

- Adding a magnifying glass to your collection will encourage the children to look even more closely at the reclaimed resources.

Delicate fingers

In the EYFS

The following statements are taken from the Practice Guidance for the EYFS, Physical Development (Using Equipment and Materials).

- Provide equipment and resources that are sufficient, challenging and interesting, and that can be used in a variety of ways, or to support specific skills.

- Give sufficient time for children to use a range of equipment, to persist in activities, practising new and exciting skills.

- (Children) begin to make and manipulate objects and tools.

Starting points

All babies and children need an environment that will stimulate their natural curiosity and their keen desire to learn about the world around them.

From a very early age, babies are intrigued by unusual resources that are provided for them to handle and manipulate. When introducing reclaimed materials to small children, safety is of prime importance. However, it is possible to introduce unusual objects in the nursery when children are supported by an attentive adult.

For babies, you can provide:
- pieces of coloured acetate
- doilies and lacy fabrics
- picnic bowls, tumblers and plates
- netting.

For toddlers and older children, you can add:
- glass nuggets
- translucent objects – plastic shapes and buttons
- translucent plastic jewellery
- polished pebbles.

Learning and development

In a day nursery, the babies and young children all have access to appropriate sized light boxes and a variety of mirrored equipment. These items of equipment fascinate the children and encourage them to develop their physical skills, as well as their creativity and critical thinking, as they choose and use reclaimed materials.

The practitioners in the nursery explain to the children why safety is important in using the equipment and handling the materials.

The baby room houses a large light box which is placed on the floor and which can be used by the babies when they choose. Reclaimed resources are offered to the children each day by the practitioners. Large place mats resembling doilies are of great interest to the seated babies, who often pull themselves up to look more closely at the effects of the mats on the light box.

The older babies are interested in the physical characteristics of the objects they encounter – they use their hands to explore and manipulate the reclaimed objects. A glass egg and pieces of acetate will have a very different 'feel' and will take on a different visual dimension when they are placed on a light box.

The older children in the nursery use reclaimed objects with the light boxes and mirrors to develop their physical dexterity and manipulation skills as they engage in exploratory play. They:

- pick the objects up and move them about
- collect the objects so that they have similar objects together
- line up the objects
- look through the objects

They develop patterns of play that identify the ways in which they prefer to explore and manipulate materials. They:

- place objects within spaces
- create patterns and pictures
- sort and classify

Other things to try

- Include reclaimed materials in treasure baskets for babies to handle – try wooden rings, wooden block offcuts, keys, buckles, chains, ribbons and perfume bottles.

- Provide toddlers with reclaimed containers, such as boxes, bags and tins, to fill with reclaimed materials, such as cotton reels, pegs, tubes and lids.

- Use reclaimed objects and a cotton drawstring bag to play 'feely' games.

Above, below and alongside

In the EYFS

The following statements are taken from the Practice Guidance for the EYFS, Physical Development (Movement and Space).

- Provide open-ended resources for large-scale building.

- Look, listen and note the way children recognise the need to take account of space when they plan to do things, such as building and demolishing a tower.

- (Children) judge body space in relation to spaces when fitting into confined spaces.

- (They) collaborate in devising and sharing tasks, including those that involve accepting rules.

Starting points

Babies and young children learn by being active and physical development takes place across all areas of learning and development. Open-ended reclaimed materials can be used to provide opportunities for children to be active and interactive, and to improve their manipulation skills, and skills of co-ordination, movement and control.

In order to engage in large-scale building with open-ended resources, young children need:

- space and opportunities to build
- time to develop their skills and interests
- attractively laid out reclaimed resources.

Learning and development

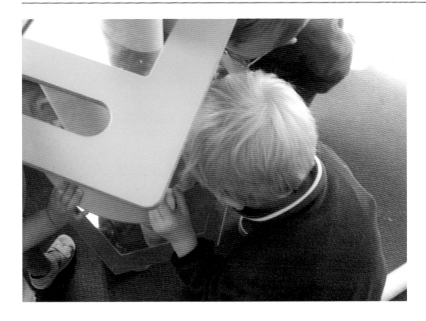

The two and a half year olds in a nursery have a wide range of reclaimed resources available to them for exploration and investigation. Constructing with the open-ended materials is a very popular activity.

The room is laid out so that there is space for the children to work collaboratively on construction projects, developing their physical skills and sense of spatial awareness. They learn how to judge their own body space and to show respect for other children's personal space as they play together.

The introduction of mirrors adds to the open-ended nature of the construction and allows the children to develop physical control, to balance and to persevere in developing new skills.

When the children move into the pre-school section of the nursery, they develop their physical and imaginative skills by making increasingly complex structures and scenes using reclaimed materials, which include:
- plastic containers
- industrial offcuts
- clear and coloured tubes and tubing
- netting
- coloured acetate
- foil 'cut out' sheets from industrial processes.

The constructions pose opportunities for the children to experience risk and challenge, and are often enhanced by the addition of fibre optic lighting, providing exciting environments for small world play and imaginative story making.

Other things to try

- Use a variety of boxes, crates and pipes to encourage large-scale construction out of doors.
- Use photographs of local landmarks to give the children ideas of what they might build.
- Talk about how to build high structures and provide opportunities for the children to climb safely when building vertically.
- Take photographs to show the children how well they are developing their physical skills.

Weaving a colourful creation

In the EYFS

The following statements are taken from the Practice Guidance for the EYFS, Creative Development (Exploring Media and Materials).

- 'Exploring Media and Materials' is about children's independent and guided exploration of, and engagement with, a widening range of media and materials, finding out about, and working with colour, texture, shape, space and form in two and three dimensions.

- Choose unusual or interesting materials and resources that inspire exploration.

- (Children) explore and begin to differentiate between colours.

- **ELG** (They) explore colour, texture, shape, form and space in two or three dimensions.

Starting points

In a room leading off from the pre-school room of a nursery, the staff have created a studio space, or atelier, where the children can explore a wide range of media and materials.

When the children expressed a growing interest in colours around them, the staff decided to provide a range of reclaimed materials as starting points that would support the children's learning. These included:

- paint colour swatches
- samples of wools and threads
- catalogues from a local art gallery.

Learning and development

The children become increasingly interested in the many different shades and tones of colours in the materials around them.

They begin to sort the materials in the studio into colours and to develop their own ideas of how to follow the practitioners' leads in displaying materials in 'palettes of colour'. A Lazy Suzy and a number of small reclaimed glass dishes are used to store items in the studio, making the resources easily accessible for children's independent exploration. These included:

- reclaimed plastic
- buttons
- mosaic pieces
- paper clips.

After looking at the artists' catalogues, two small groups of children decide they want to recreate the pictures on a large scale. They have all previously enjoyed learning to weave, so the practitioners provide reclaimed materials for the children's designs, including:

- papers
- fabrics
- wool
- foil
- ribbons
- cellophane.

Garden netting is used as frames for the weaving. The beautiful finished woven panels take several hours to complete, emphasising the importance of children having the time they need to be creative.

The children are proud of their large-scale pieces of artwork which are hung in the entrance hall of the nursery for children, parents and visitors to see and admire.

Other things to try

- Collect buttons and beads to sort into shades of different colours.
- Use cards and calendars as starting points for looking at colours in natural and built environments.
- Use an overhead projector to explore the colours of translucent reclaimed materials.
- A collection of reclaimed metal resources, such as springs, washers and bolts, will create an interesting starting point for an investigation of colour. Try placing them on a reflective tray for a special effect.

The kitchen tool band

In the EYFS

The following statements are taken from the Practice Guidance for the EYFS, Creative Development (Creating Music and Dance).

- Creating music and dance is about children's independent and guided exploration of sound, movement and music. Focusing on how sounds can be made and changed, and how they can be recognised and repeated from a pattern, this activity includes ways of exploring movement, matching movements to music and singing simple songs from memory.

- (Children) explore and learn how sounds can be changed.

Starting points

The staff of a nursery school put together a collection of reclaimed kitchen tools for the children to use both indoors and outside. The kitchen utensils have been collected by staff and families, from car boot sales and charity shops.

The kitchen utensils include:
- tools made from different materials: metal, wood and plastic
- tools with holes in them
- brushes, whisks and beaters.

Learning and development

One of the children in the nursery decides that she wants to use the kitchen tools to make music outside. She chooses a selection of tools to 'make her band' and decides that she wants to hang them up in the entrance to the nursery garden. With the help of a friend and a practitioner, the girl ties her chosen tools on to string and secures the string to the garden gates, ready to make music.

She chooses:
- metal sieves and strainers
- plastic tongs
- a wooden brush
- a metal spaghetti serving spoon.

Next, the beaters are chosen. She chooses:
- a wooden spoon
- a metal spoon
- a metal whisk.

The young musician becomes absorbed in exploring her ideas about sound, music making, rhythm and movement as she transforms the reclaimed kitchen tools into a percussion band.

Other things to try

- Provide tins, boxes and plastic bottles to make shakers that sound different. The sound they make will also be dependent on what is put inside – offer buttons, beads, corks, nuts and bolts.

- Strong elastic bands stretched around a shoebox will make a simple instrument to pluck.

- Pots and pans of different shapes and sizes will make an outdoor 'steel band'.

- A variety of reclaimed materials can be used to make wind chimes for your outdoor area.

USING NATURAL MATERIALS

What could I do with this?

In the EYFS

The following statements are taken from the Practice Guidance for the EYFS, Personal Social and Emotional Development (Dispositions and Attitudes).

- Recognise that children's interest may last for short or long periods, and that their interests and preferences vary.
- Value and support the decisions that children make. Encourage them when they try new things.
- Teach children to use and care for materials, and then trust them to do so independently.
- (Children) develop a curiosity about things and processes.
- (They) show their particular characteristics, preferences and interests.

Starting points

Natural materials are perfect resources to use in heuristic play sessions. A selection of interesting cones, pods, dried whole fruits and wicker balls provide children with many opportunities to develop their conceptual understanding of:

- big and little
- same and different
- heavy and light
- long and short
- few and many.

They also encourage early counting, matching and fitting one thing inside another.

Learning and development

In the room for two year olds in a day nursery, the practitioners have presented a large basket of natural materials to the children. They are fascinated by the materials and spend time playing individually, manipulating the contents of the basket. Two of the girls are particularly interested in the large exotic seed pods and they spend time peacefully turning over the pods in their hands, focusing their whole attention on what they are seeing and handling.

One of the girls stays with the collection of natural materials for a long period of time. She selects different items in turn, rotating them in her hands and smelling them.

She inevitably puts them in her mouth to see what they feel and taste like. She is particularly interested in 'tasting' the dried limes in the collection. Throughout this time of exploration, the child's play is focused and uninterrupted by social interaction with other children.

The boys in the group interact with the natural materials differently. They become involved in:

- picking up the objects and putting them in different places
- rolling the objects along the floor.

They enjoy:

- putting the natural resources into containers, such as boxes and tins
- emptying the natural objects out of the containers.

One boy is particularly interested in transferring objects from one container to another.

Throughout the heuristic play session, the children demonstrate their curiosity, experiment with the materials and make decisions about what they do next. Their play is self-initiated and the practitioners encourage the children to focus their attention for extended periods of time by staying peacefully in the background and not intervening in the children's play.

Using a different collection of natural materials, the older toddlers build on their past experience and knowledge as they play with the objects. They also demonstrate behaviour that is typical of heuristic play, such as banging objects together.

Once again, their heuristic play leads the children to make discoveries about the world and how it works, for example by placing smaller objects inside larger objects.

They explore the natural materials for long periods of time displaying their curiosity about each object in turn.

When one of the older girls becomes aware of the holes in a seed pod, the practitioner expresses her personal interest in the discovery, valuing the child's learning, sharing the experience with her and quietly encouraging her to try something new.

Other things to try

- Provide collections of shells, conkers or pebbles that can be slid through tubes of different types and sizes.

- Place a basket of round natural objects at the top of a slope indoors or out of doors for the children to roll.

- Provide a selection of small natural materials, such as conkers or pebbles, which can be fitted inside larger natural objects, such as bell cups or flat shells.

- Use photographs to record any patterns in the children's behaviour and use the evidence to plan the next steps in their learning.

❝Value and support the discoveries that children make and encourage them to try new things.❞

❝A sensitive practitioner will express an interest in children's discoveries, value their learning and support their exploration.❞

Where we live

In the EYFS

The following statements are taken from the Practice Guidance for the EYFS, Personal Social and Emotional Development (Sense of Community).

- Provide activities and opportunities for children to share experiences and knowledge from different parts of their lives with each other.

- Note instances of children drawing upon their experiences beyond the setting, as well as children's references to groups, people and places in the different communities of which they are members.

- (Children) make connections between different parts of their life experience.

Starting points

Natural materials, with their different sensory appeals, can be used effectively to help children to express and develop ideas, thoughts and feelings. Their open-ended nature means that they can be easily transformed in children's imagination into props for storytelling, allowing them to reflect on their own experiences.

In the autumn, a practitioner working with three and four year olds decided to see how children expressed themselves when using natural materials. Taking her influence from the educators in the pre-schools of Reggio Emilia in Italy, the practitioner decided to introduce the idea of 'wait time' by giving the children time to consider the materials she presented to them without asking them to do anything with them.

Learning and development

At the beginning of the week, the practitioner set up a table in the pre-school room with colour-coded piles of leaves, conkers, twigs and bark.

The children were very curious about the display, but also very respectful of it and they did not disrupt the piles. Throughout the week, the children looked at the natural materials on the table. On Friday, when the time came to fully present the activity to the children, they needed little encouragement to start exploring the materials as the anticipation had been building up all week.

One of the boys immediately started laying out twigs confidently and methodically onto his paper and, when he had no more twigs, he added conkers. He seemed to be making choices, filling spaces and, at the end of the process, he had created a beautifully arranged composition.

'This is my garden' he said.

A second boy picked out a large leaf from the selection available and placed conkers on it. Then he found a second leaf and put it on top, saying, *'I'm building a castle.'*

When a photograph was taken of the completed castle, he asked for a second to be taken *'of the inside'* and he took the top leaf off.

After watching the boys for some time, one of the girls filled a plastic pot with all the conkers she could find and said, *'I'm trying to build mummy's house.'*

She covered the house with a leaf *'to keep it warm.'*

A second girl in the group found another pot to put on top, saying, *'It's gone home now.'*

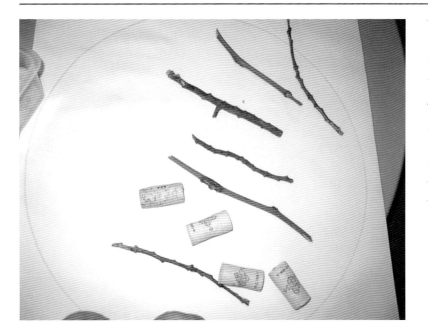

The children showed a strong narrative approach to the natural materials, linking their arrangements to different parts of their life experiences.

The practitioner then presented the three and four year olds with white sheets of paper on which a faint circle was drawn. She was interested to see whether or not the boundary would influence the way the children arranged the natural materials.

Most of the children made their compositions inside the circle, but some ignored it completely. As they worked, the children talked about what they were creating and a common theme began to emerge. The twigs and corks represented trees and plants in the local park. Tissue paper shapes and conkers became the playground equipment as the children talked about visiting the park at the weekend with their families.

One of the boys began by balancing corks on top of each other and said,
'This is a street and these are the towers.'

He picked up a blue tissue square and said, *'I need blue ones for the sea, one, two, three, four, we need four countries',* as he counted the edges of the square. The rest of the group watched closely as he placed ribbons on his picture. *'These are the roads and these are the ends of the roads. This is Streatham Common.'*

He then paused for a moment before saying, *'This is going to be a city. These are the paths that go all the different ways. Some go to Australia.'*

Finally, he drew his thinking back to the community in which he and the other children lived. He put corks on the tissue paper shapes and announced, *'These could be more things in the swing park. You could roll on them.'*

By providing a range of open-ended natural materials that the children could supplement with other resources, the practitioner gave them the opportunity to develop their thoughts and ideas about the community in which they lived. At the same time, the boy constructing a 'city' was able to work through his personal theories about maps, cities, construction and even whole countries and continents.

Other things to try

- Take groups of children for walks in the local community and look at the natural world around you.

- Provide 'collectors' bags' for the children to collect natural materials from the area where they live so that they can use them in your setting.

- Invite the parents or grandparents of the children in your group to talk to the children about gardening, flower and plant arranging or about how they used sticks, stones, shells or conkers as toys when they were small.

- Ask the children's families to help make a collection or display of unusual natural objects. They may have some from other parts of the world that will add to the interest.

Sea creature story

In the EYFS

The following statements are taken from the Practice Guidance for the EYFS, Communication, Language and Literacy (Language for Communication).

- Foster children's enjoyment of spoken and written language by providing interesting and stimulating play opportunities.

- Note how children link statements to develop stories and explanations.

- (Children) consistently develop a simple story line, explanation or line of questioning.

- ELG (They) interact with others, negotiating plans and activities and taking turns in conversation.

Starting points

Water is one of the most easily available natural materials. Freezing the water and using ice cubes to enhance small world play provides an interesting and stimulating environment for children to develop their language for communication.

The practitioners in a pre-school placed a large tray filled with ice cubes in the outdoor area for the children to encounter. Alongside the ice cubes they provided a range of natural and man-made objects – shells, a wooden boat, good quality plastic sea creatures and a turtle soap dish. They chose a bright day in Winter when there was less likelihood of the ice cubes melting before the children had time to engage in conversations with one another.

Learning and development

Three girls approached the tray of ice cubes and eagerly began to explore the tray and its contents, readily engaging in conversation about what they could see and what they were doing.

They looked at each of the objects in the tray, expressing delight as they handled the cold shells and other resources. The girls took turns in the conversation, attentively listening to what the others had to say.

As they handled the ice cubes they talked about how cold they felt and how cold their hands were. They used a wide range of vocabulary describing temperature, texture, change and how they were feeling.

Presented with the same resources, two of the girls showed very different interests. One of the girls was intrigued by the ice cubes themselves, eagerly explaining to the others what she knew about making ice cubes and describing what happens when ice melts.

The younger girl began to tell a story about the turtle 'boat' carrying ice cubes across the sea.

She introduced the sea creatures as characters in her story, describing how they had come to help the turtle carry the ice to the other side of the world.

The shells became small boats which were also carrying the ice away. Each of the shell boats had one ice cube placed inside it before starting on a long journey.

The other girls then joined in the story, picking up on the characters and story line which had been developed.

The practitioner recorded the experience with the ice cubes in a series of photographs and notes of the children's conversations. These were then shared with the children and made into a book which included the story of the journey of the turtle boat and an explanation of how ice is formed and what happens to it when it melts.

Other things to try

- Use ice cubes alongside small world play to encourage children to re-enact familiar stories set in cold climates.

- Introduce rhymes and songs which have a 'cold' theme.

- Make a set of instructions with the children which show the sequence of events in making ice cubes and watching them melt.

- Provide a word bank of 'hot and cold' words for the children to use.

"Foster children's enjoyment of spoken and written language by providing interesting and stimulating play opportunities."

"The practitioner plays a key role in recording children's experiences in photographs and in notes of the children's conversations."

Experiences to remember

In the EYFS

The following statements are taken from the Practice Guidance for the EYFS, Communication, Language and Literacy (Language for Thinking).

- Set up shared experiences that children can reflect upon.

- Note how children use talk to reflect upon, clarify, sequence and think about present and past experiences, ideas and feelings.

- (Children) begin to make patterns in their experience through linking cause and effect, sequencing, ordering and grouping.

- ELG (They) use talk to organise, sequence and clarify thinking, ideas, feelings and events.

Starting points

By providing a wide range of natural materials in their setting, practitioners can support and challenge children's thinking, enabling them to make connections in their learning. A creative learning environment can be enhanced by:

- displaying a selection of natural materials attractively as part of the everyday environment. Children can access the natural resources, changing the order and sequence of the display.

- using trays and mats to display collections of natural materials that will encourage the children to explore and investigate.

- placing natural objects on a mirrored surface to encourage the children to think critically about what they can see and to speculate on what is 'real' and 'not real'.

Learning and development

Collections of natural materials are used in a nursery to encourage the children to think critically and to develop their language for thinking. The collections vary in size and content, and are stored in wicker hampers, wooden boxes and interesting reclaimed containers to complement the beauty of the natural materials.

The children are encouraged to work collaboratively with the collections and they often choose to use neutral table mats as a base for placing and arranging the objects they are interested in. Three of the four year olds have decided to explore one of the smaller collections of natural materials together.

The boy in the group selects a shell from the box. He looks closely at the shell, turning it round and round and commenting on the spiral effect he is creating. Meanwhile, the girls choose different objects and begin placing and arranging them on the table mat. They use positional language as they talk about the arrangements they are creating.

The boy tells the girls that they can hear the sea if they listen to a shell because he has tried it before. He suggests that they should all try listening to the sea in his shell and holds it up for the child next to him to listen.

The three children select natural objects from the box in turn. They talk about what they are holding, what they think each item is and express their feelings about the objects, their preferences, likes and dislikes.

Two of the children spend over half an hour engaging in sustained shared thinking as they explore the natural materials with all their senses, talking about things they have seen before. The smells of the natural materials are particularly evocative and the children recall similar smells they have encountered in the past. They reminisce about family outings and events in the nursery where they have experienced the smell and texture of natural materials.

They find great pleasure in predicting which of the natural materials they can balance on their noses and why!

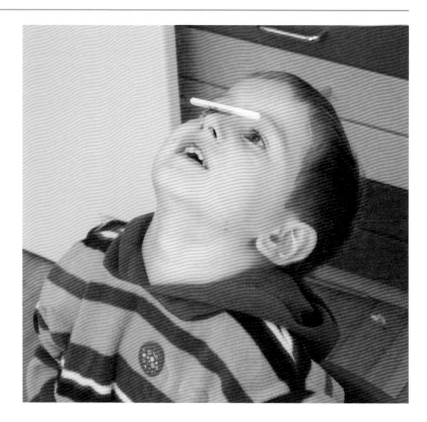

Other things to try

- Set up displays of photographs of natural materials taken from unusual angles. Ask the children to describe what they are seeing.

- Use natural objects inside a feely bag to encourage the children to talk about what they can feel, to make comparisons with objects they are familiar with and to guess what is in the bag.

- Include natural materials in small world play for the children to re-enact stories and events.

- Use collections of natural materials for sorting and classifying. Ask the children to explain why they have sorted the natural materials in the ways they have chosen.

"The smells of natural materials are particularly evocative and enable children to recall similar smells they have encountered in the past."

Numbers indoors and out

In the EYFS

The following statements are taken from the Practice Guidance for the EYFS, Problem Solving, Reasoning and Numeracy (Numbers as Labels and for Counting).

- Note situations that prompt children to talk about numbers.

- Note instances of children counting an irregular arrangement of up to ten objects.

- (Children) count actions or objects that cannot be moved.

- (They) estimate how many objects they can see and check by counting them.

Starting points

Providing collections of natural materials for children to sort, order, count and label in their play will enhance a setting's provision for mathematical development.

Baskets of stones, shells and cones are beautiful to look at and aesthetically pleasing to handle.

Learning and development

The practitioners in a day nursery noticed that the 3 year olds were very interested in counting natural materials. They arranged their environment so that a range of natural materials were easily accessible to the children alongside sorting trays and mark-making equipment.

One of the girls became fascinated by a collection of pods and stones. She selected a tray which was divided into compartments and began placing a natural object in each of the spaces, counting the objects as she went along.

Her attention was then caught by a head of Indian corn. She began to count the individual kernels, counting reliably up to ten and then using larger numbers at random to complete the task.

By observing closely, the girl's key person was able to build on her understanding of one-to-one correspondence, her ability to count to ten and her interest in counting larger quantities. The practitioner found another head of corn, sat next to the girl and modelled counting using numbers beyond ten.

Having observed the children counting natural materials indoors, the practitioners decided that they would focus their attention on observing the children counting in the garden.

One of the practitioners noticed a group of children counting the daisies in the lawn. One of the boys counted the daisies as he picked them, saying a number name for each of the daisies he picked.

A discussion ensued about whether or not they should be picking the daisies, even if they wanted to count them. A second boy showed the others how to count the daisies without actually picking each one. He very effectively demonstrated that he could count objects that could not be moved.

The children continued walking around the garden together, finding different flowers to count. The boy who had insisted on picking the daisies in order to count them, now showed that he could count irregular arrangements of natural 'objects' up to, and beyond, ten.

The group then posed themselves the challenge of counting the petals of the flowers. They spent an extended period of time in the garden estimating how many petals they could see and then counting them to check if they were right.

The practitioner's awareness of the opportunities to observe the children counting as they played out of doors enabled her to build on the children's interests and to use observational assessment to plan the next stages in their learning.

Other things to try

- Use themed collections of stones, cones, twigs or shells to encourage children to sort and classify objects.

- Take photographs of natural materials in different sized groups to create a number line.

- Encourage the children to use natural materials as props in transactional play – as items for sale, as money or as weights with a set of scales.

- Provide number labels and mark making materials outdoors for the children to represent their counting and calculations.

❝Collections of natural materials to sort, order and classify enhance a setting's provision for mathematical learning.❞

Solving problems outdoors

In the EYFS

The following statements are taken from the Practice Guidance for the EYFS, Problem Solving, Reasoning and Numeracy (Calculating).

- Show interest in how children solve problems and value their different solutions.

- Note the methods children use to answer a problem they have posed.

- (Children) use their own methods to work through a problem.

ELG In practical activities and discussion, they begin to use the vocabulary involved in adding and subtracting.

Starting points

With a little imagination and creative thought the outdoor environment can incorporate a mathematical component, providing a wealth of opportunities to encourage children's mathematical problem solving.

Murals on walls, the arrangements of paved areas, as well as sand and water areas can all help foster children's interest in finding and solving problems.

Learning and development

In the nursery unit of a school the practitioners have created a wonderful sensory garden which provides endless opportunities for learning and development across all six areas of learning in the EYFS.

A small water feature with a fountain inside a barrel was added to the garden to enhance the outdoor provision for the children. For safety reasons the water and fountain were covered by a metal grid and an assortment of large pebbles.

The children became interested, not only in the fountain and how it behaved, but also the ways in which they could use the grid and pebbles to create and solve mathematical problems.

One of the first problems the children posed was how to stop the water from bubbling out from the fountain. They predicted how many pebbles they would need and where they would need to place them.

The children talked about how they would solve the problem. They used vocabulary involved in adding and subtracting as they worked together. Their discussions involved the use of positional language as they re-positioned the pebbles on the metal grid, making sure that each square on the grid had one pebble placed upon it.

'Get one more pebble and put it beside this one.'
'Take one away from this side and move it over.'
'We need two more to make six in this row.'

The children went on to record their solutions to the problem they had posed by drawing a grid and showing where they had placed the pebbles on the grid in relation to the fountain.

In another area of the sensory garden the children and practitioners created a 3-D mural also based upon a grid design.

The children decided to use natural materials from their local area to create their wall design. They selected a variety of stones, shells and string as well as adding mirrors and corks for added interest.

The mural was used on a regular basis for counting and mathematical problem solving. On some occasions this was practitioner-led when new concepts and vocabulary could be introduced. At other times the children chose to pose, and solve, their own mathematical problems either individually or as part of a small group.

Other things to try

- Create a 3-D number line mural out of doors using natural materials.
- Play addition and subtraction games using a selection of natural materials.
- Encourage children to share out pebbles or shells equally among their group.
- Use collections of natural materials alongside a range of mirrors to pose problems for the children to solve.

Leaves that come and go

In the EYFS

The following statements are taken from the Practice Guidance for the EYFS, Knowledge and Understanding of the World (Time).

- Make use of outdoor areas to give opportunities for investigations of the natural world.
- Provide opportunities to record findings by, for example, drawing, writing, making a model or photographing.
- (Children) show an awareness of change.
- (They) understand about the seasons of the year and their regularity.
- (They) show curiosity and interest in the features of objects and living things.

Starting points

Using natural materials indoors can be a useful starting point for arousing children's interest in the natural world around them, encouraging them to want to know more about the features of living things.

In a day nursery, the three and four year olds were provided with a wide range of natural materials to investigate and use to develop their interests and learning. An interest in leaves – where they are found, what they look and feel like, how they change over time – arose from an arrangement created by one of the children. The arrangement was made by placing skeleton leaves and other natural materials on a black tile, which was surrounded by a silver picture frame.

Learning and development

The structure and patterns of the delicate skeleton leaves fascinated the children, who then explored the outdoor environment in search of similar leaves. They spent time outside, looking under the trees and making connections between the different leaf types and trees from which they had fallen.

The practitioners encouraged the leaf search and added to the interest and excitement by providing torches so that the children could explore in the garden before going home in the early evening.

They talked to the children about night and day, the changing seasons and how some trees lose their leaves in autumn before growing new ones in the spring.

The children collected a variety of leaves which they took indoors to use in leaf printing and picture making. The practitioners kept the leaves that the children had used to create a display, showing both the prints and the actual leaves.

The staff had also recorded the actual words the children used when they were investigating the leaves so that they could begin to have an understanding of what the children were thinking:

'But the leaves are all dirty so we could paint them.'
'You need to make all the different colours for the leaves – browns and greens.'
'Different greens.'
'We added blue to make the leaves darker.'

The children's fascination for the leaves was reawakened the following spring when the new leaves appeared on the trees in the garden. They were still intrigued by the structures of the skeleton leaves, which they viewed on a light box indoors.

The practitioners showed the children how to make rubbings of leaves from the trees in the garden, talking to them about the patterns they could see emerging as they worked.

By chance, an indoor plant had lost all of its leaves through not having been watered. The children were very concerned about the situation and talked at length about what should be done to help the plant.

The first thing they did was to name the plant 'Terry the Tree', as they felt that they had let down a good friend. They then talked about how they could provide Terry with some new leaves. Different children had different ideas about what would work best to make the new leaves. Some of the children set about carefully creating leaves from rubbings on white paper.

Others felt that brown paper cut into leaf shapes worked. Those children who felt that Terry needed to be cheered up chose coloured cellophane for their leaves.

Finally, the leaves were attached to Terry the Tree, and the children felt that they had done a good job in restoring the tree to its former glory.

The 'Terry the Tree' project gave the children the opportunity to share, and develop their knowledge and understanding of trees, leaves and seasonal change. As they talked about why the plant had died, they became aware of the need to care for living things and to understand cause and effect in the natural world.

Other things to try

- Draw the children's attention to the patterns found on leaves, bark, shells and stones.

- Encourage the children to use magnifiers and fine drawing pencils to produce close observational drawings of leaves and other natural materials.

- Experiment with the way leaves fall from a height. Talk about the ways in which they fall to the ground. Do they all fall the same way?

- Use skeleton leaves as starting points to talk about the human skeleton and those of other living things.

Looking closely

In the EYFS

The following statements are taken from the Practice Guidance for the EYFS, Knowledge and Understanding of the World (Exploration and Investigation).

- Provide opportunities to observe things closely through a variety of means, including magnifiers and photographs.

- Note how children examine objects and living things to find out more about them, and the ways in which children find out about things in the environment, for example, by handling something and looking at it closely.

- **ELG** (Children) investigate objects and materials by using all of their senses as appropriate.

- **ELG** (They) find out about, and identify, some features of living things, objects and events they observe.

Starting points

Young children are often acutely aware of the natural world around them. They are fascinated by what plants and flowers look like close up, and frequently look closely at the similarities, differences and patterns they find.

In order to encourage young children to look closely at the natural world, it is important to provide them with the appropriate tools that will help them to look closely as they explore and investigate.

Using a hand-held magnifier is a skill that has to be learned in order for children to know how to find the correct focal length, to observe objects close up. Younger children will find it easier to use a stand magnifier or a simple sheet magnifier to examine natural objects.

Placing natural materials on a light box also helps children to see the details of their shapes, patterns and structures.

Learning and development

In a children's centre, the practitioners created a display of fruits and seed pods for the children to explore and investigate. The natural materials were set out attractively on a millstone in the outside area, creating a focused environment for close observation.

The children were encouraged to investigate the natural materials using hand-held magnifiers and sheet magnifiers. They were very interested in handling the natural materials and looking at them closely. The practitioners responded to the children's signs of interest by adding to the variety of pods and fruits on the millstone.

One of the youngest three year old girls was particularly interested in looking closely using a magnifier. She spent an extended period of time selecting individual objects and looking at them through the lens.

She gradually became more and more efficient at holding the hand lens in the correct position to enable her to see the detail of the seed pods.

After 15 minutes, an older girl approached the investigation area and began to copy the younger girl's actions, eventually mastering the correct positioning of the hand lens for herself.

By taking photographs of the three year old's developing competence with the hand lens, the practitioner was later able to talk to her about how much she had achieved.

Other things to try

- Create interactive displays with natural materials placed under a stand magnifier or behind a sheet magnifier placed on its edge.

- Cut fruits and vegetables in half lengthways and encourage the children to look closely at them, describing what they see.

- Take close-up photographs of the natural materials in your setting and encourage the children to match them with the real thing.

- Take photographs of the detail of natural materials in your outdoor environment and encourage the children to find the real objects.

Moving pumpkins

> ## In the EYFS
>
> The following statements are taken from the Practice Guidance for the EYFS, Physical Development (Movement and Space).
>
> - Provide novelty in the environment that encourages babies to use all of their senses and move indoors and outdoors.
>
> - Note what babies like to try to reach for and play with, and the skills they develop.
>
> - (Babies) make strong and purposeful movements, often moving from the position in which they are placed.
>
> - (They) use their increasing mobility to connect with toys, objects and people.

Starting points

Autumn is an ideal time of year to introduce new and unusual natural materials to babies. Pumpkins, gourds and squashes are attractive resources because of the way they look, feel and move.

In the baby room of a day nursery, the babies' key persons decide to introduce a selection of pumpkins, squashes and gourds of different shapes, sizes and colours. They place them in one of the babies' favourite areas of the room, next to the large triptych mirror.

Learning and development

Two of the babies show a particular interest in the natural resources. They crawl towards them and begin to pick them up, starting with the smaller yellow squashes.

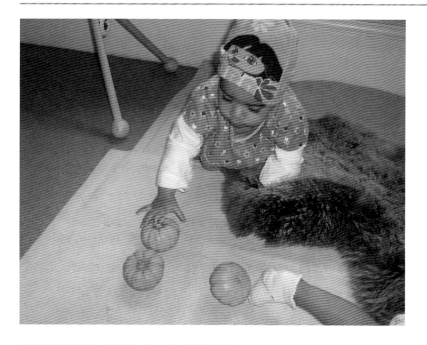

One of the babies reaches out to touch each of the squashes in turn gently. She then carefully watches what happens when she pushes them, making them move.

The other baby turns her attention to the pumpkins, feeling their shape and touching the remains of the stalks.

The baby co-ordinates her movements in order to be in a position to try lifting one of the pumpkins. She delightedly shows her key person her skill in lifting a heavy object. The practitioner responds by praising her achievement.

During the morning, the pumpkins, squashes and gourds continue to interest the babies in different ways. They move the natural objects by lifting, pushing and rolling them around on the floor. They line them up, place them next to the mirror and move them away from the area.

After the children had had their lunch and a sleep, the practitioners found that the babies were no longer interested in the pumpkins, squashes and gourds, so they decided to move them away from the triptych mirror to another part of the room. They placed the natural materials in another of the babies' favourite spots, inside an alcove.

The baby who had played for the longest with the pumpkins during the morning session immediately headed for the alcove and resumed her exploration, focusing her attention on the small squashes this time.

She was soon noticed by her original playmate, who crawled over to join her and they continued to investigate the squashes and pumpkins peacefully together.

The re-presenting of the natural materials to the babies in a different context reawakened their interest and natural curiosity.

When the same collection of pumpkins, squashes and gourds were presented to the toddlers, they were approached in a very different way. Two of the boys decided to take a basket of the natural objects to the top of the indoor slide. They became very excited as they explored the patterns of movement made by rolling the squashes down a slope...

...and down the stairs.

The children's key persons were able to anticipate the children's continuing exuberance and made sure that the space around the slide was kept clear while the toddlers carried out their investigations.

Other things to try

- Place pumpkins, squashes and gourds on different surfaces – carpet, wood, grass – so that the children can explore how they move.

- Play games with the children that involve rolling, dropping or catching appropriate natural objects.

- Try presenting the same natural objects to the children at different times over a period of a week to see if they build on their learning and skill development each day.

- Observe the children as they play with the natural objects to see if particular patterns of movement, or schemas, occur.

Pick it up

In the EYFS

The following statements are taken from the Practice Guidance for the EYFS, Physical Development (Using Equipment and Materials).

- Provide tweezers, tongs and small scoops for use in play and investigation.

- Note the variety of skills children use to manipulate materials and objects, such as picking up, releasing, threading and posting.

- (Children) use one-handed tools and equipment.

- **ELG** (They) handle tools, objects, construction and markable materials safely and with increasing control.

Starting points

Activities that involve separating mixtures provide an interesting challenge for children and adults alike.

In a family workshop at a nursery school, one of the activities involved inviting children and their parents to use a variety of sieves, scoops, tongs and chopsticks to separate mixtures of dried pulses, lentils, rice and sand set out in trays and wooden boxes.

Learning and development

The family workshop provided an ideal opportunity for children and their parents to share their ideas, skills and expertise when using the tools provided to separate the mixtures of natural materials.

The adults were able to model their skills for the children, who were very keen to try out new manipulative skills for themselves.

The adults were willing to follow the children's ideas, watching their strategies for using the tools to solve the challenge, and praising their skills.

As they investigated the natural materials and the tools together, the children and their parents talked about using tools, such as chopsticks, safely. The adults spent time teaching their children how to use the tools effectively and safely.

Onlookers also paid attention to the different adults' skills and proceeded to copy their actions. Some of the children were very persistent as they purposefully practised handling the tools with increasing control.

Some of the children were particularly creative in finding solutions to their problems. One of the boys in the nursery was joined at the family workshop by his mother and younger brother. As a family group, they soon became very interested in the separating mixtures activity.

The older boy was encouraged by his mother to try using the chopsticks to lift the dried butter beans out of the mixture in the tray. His younger brother seemed to be adept at moving the beans around using a set of wooden tongs.

When the older boy moved on to a different activity, and the adult's attention moved away from what he was doing, it became apparent that his younger sibling had found an enterprising solution to the difficulties he was encountering with using the tongs.

He used his fine motor skills to good effect – picking up the butter beans, pinching them between his fingers and thumb, squeezing the tongs together and holding them in position as he moved the butter beans from one place to another in the tray. A very successful and creative strategy!

Other things to try

- Provide treasure baskets of natural materials for non-mobile babies to handle and manipulate.

- Use a range of natural materials in heuristic play sessions with toddlers.

- Provide sticks, cones, wicker balls, large shells or stones to use in dough, clay or sand.

- Encourage the children to talk about how they are using natural materials, suggesting vocabulary such as 'lift', 'touch', 'feel', 'drop', 'collect' or 'move'.

"Note the variety of skills children use to manipulate materials and objects."

Representing flowers

In the EYFS

The following statements are taken from the Practice Guidance for the EYFS, Creative Development (Exploring Media and Materials).

- Make time and space for children to express their curiosity and explore the environment using all of their senses.

- Provide a wide range of materials, resources and sensory experiences to enable children to explore colour, texture and space. Document the processes children go through to create their own 'work'.

- Provide children with opportunities to use their skills and explore concepts and ideas through their representations.

- (Children) understand that they can use lines to enclose a space, and then begin to use these shapes to represent objects.

- (They) understand that different media can be combined to create new effects.

Starting points

By providing a range of media and materials for children for children to choose from, both indoors and outdoors, practitioners can foster children's interest in natural materials in the world around them.

The children in a nursery group have been looking closely at plants, flowers, leaves, cones and seeds in the nursery garden throughout the year.

Learning and development

The practitioners in the nursery have provided clipboards with good quality drawing paper and a selection of crayons and paints for the children to use. Some stems of blossom which the children had noticed growing in the garden have been laid out on the outdoor tables as a provocation, or stimulus, for the children's creative activity.

A group of boys are particularly interested in the blossom and two of the boys begin to use the crayons to portray their images of the flowers and leaves.

The two boys are closely watched by a third boy who is fascinated by the drawings which are emerging. He watches silently as one of the boys adds detail to his picture for quite some time. At this stage he is happy to watch what is happening and the practitioner gives him time to observe the drawing process without pressing him to begin drawing himself.

Later, the practitioner joins another boy who is showing interest in the blossom. She talks to him about what he can see, introducing vocabulary to help him to express his observations such as 'shiny', 'prickly', 'rough', 'smooth' 'patterned' or 'jagged'.

The practitioner uses photography to record the processes the children go through when creating their drawings. She can share the photographs with the children, with parents and with colleagues as they plan what experiences to offer the children next.

Portraying the 'white' blossom on white paper creates an interesting challenge to the children and encourages them to look closely at the actual colours they can see in the detail of the flowers.

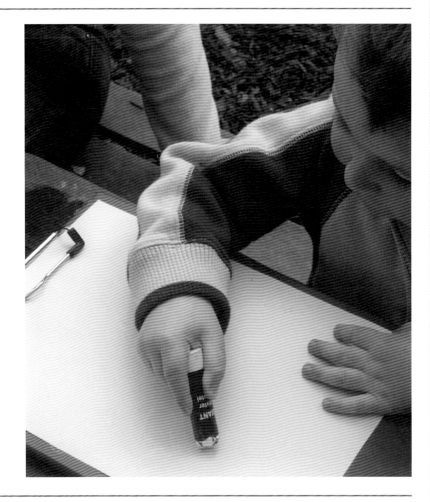

The children demonstrate acute concentration as they become engrossed in drawing the natural materials. In this nursery, the practitioners have found that drawing and painting out of doors attracts boys to representational mark making.

One of the older boys experiments with the different ways in which he can use the crayons. He uses the ends and the sides of the crayons to create different effects.

He follows this up by adding paint to his original drawing, showing that he understands that different media can be combined to create new effects and textures.

Later in the week, the children develop their interest in flowers and leaves by looking closely at photographs which they had taken of the blossom in the garden. The close up images enable the children to look very closely at the shapes and patterns of the flower heads.

Some of the children choose to use fine pencils and pens to represent the flowers. Others use palettes of paint and fine paint brushes which allow them to paint the detail of what they see.

Two of the girls make close observational drawings using a combination of fine felt-tipped pens and paint.

In whatever way they have decided to represent the blossom and flowers, all the children have shown how capable they are of selecting their own materials and how confident they are in finding their own way of representing what they see.

Other things to try

- Encourage the children to use magnifying lenses to look closely at natural materials.

- Make 'still life' arrangements of cones, pods, twigs, driftwood for the children to draw.

- Provide a wide range of fine drawing pencils, pens, charcoal and pastels for the children to make representations of natural materials.

- Cut fruit and vegetables in half lengthways and talk to the children about how to represent the detail of the cross sections they see.

- Encourage children to represent natural materials using different media, including collage, fabric work or appropriate construction materials.

Starting with a snail

In the EYFS

The following statements are taken from the Practice Guidance for the EYFS, Creative Development (Being Creative: Responding to Experiences, and Expressing and Communicating Ideas).

- Look, listen and note how children design and create, either using their own ideas or by developing those of others.
- Encourage children to discuss and appreciate beauty around them in nature and the environment.
- Ensure that there is enough time for children to express their thoughts, ideas and feelings in a variety of ways.
- (Children) develop preferences for forms of expression.
- **ELG** (They) respond in a variety of ways to what they see, hear, smell, touch and feel.

Starting points

By encouraging the children to look closely at the natural world around them, practitioners can encourage them to respond to new experiences by communicating their ideas and thoughts, and expressing them using various representational styles.

In a day nursery, children of all ages are accustomed to spending time out of doors where they enjoy drawing and painting. The practitioners encourage the children to look closely at the natural world around them, representing what they see in a variety of media.

Learning and development

On a sunny day, the practitioners set up the outdoor picnic tables as a painting area where the children can access paper and painting materials whenever they want to.

To everyone's surprise, a snail begins to move across a blank piece of paper, causing a great deal of interest and excitement. The children can see the shape of the snail very clearly as it moves slowly over the white surface. They talk quietly about its shape, its shadow, its movements and the trail it left behind it.

A small group of children are enthralled by the snail. They watch it intently, whispering to one another about what they can see. They are particularly intrigued by the shape of its shell and the movement of its feelers.

The practitioner suggests that they could look more closely at the snail if they made a temporary home for it in a glass container. The children are able to look at the underside of the snail as well as looking very closely at the shell using a hand lens. This also provides the practitioner with the opportunity to talk about taking care of living things and ensuring that the snail comes to no harm.

After discussion with the practitioner, the children talk about the different ways in which they could represent the shape of the snail. Some of the children carry on painting their images, showing the tracks the snail made.

Others return indoors and use thick paint, brushes and their fingers to create the outlines of spirals.

The practitioner shows the children how to make a print of their design by placing absorbent paper on top of their representation, creating negative and positive images.

The rest of the group, who had been observing the snail, decide to use pipe cleaners to create 3D representations of the snail, twisting the pipe cleaners around their fingers.

They create spiral outlines on sheets of paper – all different ways of expressing what they have seen and their ideas about snails and spirals.

Other things to try

The children in a Reception class also found inspiration from looking at snails and went on to produce some very sophisticated pictures and designs based on their experience. The practitioner displayed the children's work beautifully, showing the level of sophistication that young children can achieve when their creative expression is guided and supported by a knowledgeable adult.

The practitioner encouraged the children to:

- look closely at a collection of shells.

- make close observational drawings using pencil and charcoal.

- use fine brushes and good quality paints to produce detailed paintings.

- use paper, card, fabric, buttons and beads to make collage spirals.

- create large-scale 3D spirals using paper cups.

- take photographs of spirals in the built environment.

Have a look outside. Where can you see spirals?

The reception children have made their own spiral designs.

Other Information

Books and publications

The Early Years Foundation Stage: Setting the Standards for Learning, Development and Care for Children from Birth to Five
DfES 00012-2007PCK-EN

The Little Book of Treasureboxes, Linda Thornton and Pat Brunton (2006) Featherstone Education

Understanding the Reggio Approach, Linda Thornton and Pat Brunton, 2nd Edition (2009) David Fulton Publishers

Bringing the Reggio Approach to Your Early Years Practice, Linda Thornton and Pat Brunton (2007) Routledge

Beautiful Stuff: Learning with Found Materials, Cathy Weisman Topal and Lella Gandini (1999) Davis Publications Inc., Worcester, Mass.

In the Spirit of the Studio: Learning from the Atelier of Reggio Emilia, Lella Gandini, Lynn T Hill, Louise Boyd Cadwell and Charles Schwall (2005) Teachers' College Press.

Resources

Information on the location of creative recycling centres and scrapstores can be found at **www.bigeyedowl.co.uk/equipment_and_craft.htm**

Baskets, boxes, table mats, trays and *Lazy Suzy* can be found in IKEA.

Reflections on Learning sell light boxes, hand-held mirrors, triptych mirrors, baskets, magnifiers, skeleton leaves and collections of natural materials.
www.reflectionsonlearning.co.uk 01732 225850.